THE WORLD OF CITIZENSHIP

J F Aylett

Hodder & Stoughton

A MEMBER OF THE HODDER HEADLINE GROUP

Acknowledgements

The publishers would like to thank the following for permission to reproduce copyright photographs in this book:
Hulton-Deutsch Collection Ltd. p4, 38; Sally and Richard Greenhill p11, 19; Ross-Parry Picture Agency p16; Zefa Picture Library p18; Public Information Office, House of Commons p24; Topham Picture Source p26; Greenpeace Communications Ltd. p30; European Parliament p32; Royal National Lifeboat Institution p43; J Allan Cash Photolibrary p44; RSPCA p31.

The publishers would like to thank the following for permission to reproduce material in this book:
The Home Office for the Neighbourhood Watch leaflet; Conservative Central Office for the extract from the Conservative manifesto, 1992; Norwich Union Life Insurance Society for the portion of their advertisement on page 47.

Every effort has been made to trace and acknowledge ownership of copyright. The publishers will be glad to make suitable arrangements with any copyright holders whom it has not been possible to contact.

British Library Cataloguing in Publication Data

Aylett, J. F.
World of Citizenship
I. Title
323.6

ISBN 0 340 56379 6

First published 1993
Impression number 10 9 8 7 6 5 4 3 2 1
Year 1988 1997 1996 1995 1994 1993

Typeset by Multiplex Techniques Ltd, Orpington, Kent.
Printed in Great Britain for Hodder & Stoughton Educational, a division of Hodder Headline PLC, Mill Road, Dunton Green, Sevenoaks, Kent TN13 2YA by St Edmundsbury Press, Bury St Edmunds, Suffolk.

Contents

1 Citizens all

KEY *words*
citizen right responsibility politician nation dictator monarchy republic monarch democracy

A citizen is a person who is a member of a nation. So every human being in the world is a citizen of some country or other. The country's government gives them certain rights. In return, it expects them to be loyal, especially in wartime.

You do not have to be a citizen of the country you were born in. If you have a British parent, it doesn't matter where you were born: you may still be a British citizen.

But some people actually choose to become a citizen of a country they were not born in. The photograph below shows people waiting to enter the United States in 1900. They could, of course, just be going there to work. But most of them also wanted to become citizens of the United States.

Why should they want to do this? There are many reasons. Some thought they stood a better chance of getting a good job in America. Others wanted to live there because the United States offered them more rights than their homeland did.

The rights you have depend on what your country chooses to give you. And, in the end, that depends on the politicians who run your country. They can give you extra rights – or they can take away your rights.

Job sheet

Please work in pairs.

1 a) What rights do you have at school or college?
b) What responsibilities do you have?
c) Are there any extra rights or responsibilities you think you should have? Be ready to make out a case for these to put to the class.

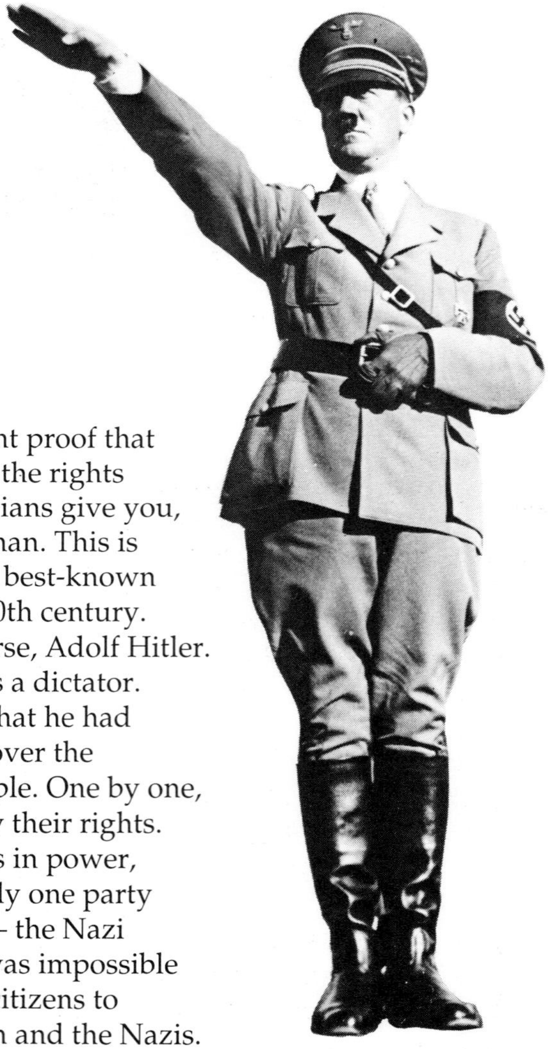

If you want proof that you only get the rights which politicians give you, look at this man. This is probably the best-known man of the 20th century. He is, of course, Adolf Hitler.

Hitler was a dictator. This means that he had total power over the German people. One by one, he took away their rights. While he was in power, there was only one party in Germany – the Nazi Party. So it was impossible for German citizens to get rid of him and the Nazis.

Some people, such as Jews, lost all their rights in Nazi Germany. During the second world war, about $5\frac{1}{2}$ million Jews were killed in concentration camps. They included children and young people.

Under Hitler's rule, Germany was a dictatorship. Today, it is a democracy. This means that the government is controlled by its citizens. Of course, you can't have millions of people meeting each time the government has to make a decision. So they have elections. These give citizens the chance to choose the politicians who will run the country.

What, you may be wondering, has this got to do with you? After all, Hitler died years ago. You are mostly British citizens, not German ones. And Britain is a democracy, not a dictatorship.

The answer was given on page 4. Politicians can give you rights – and take them away. Just because you have rights now doesn't mean you will always have them. There is no guarantee that Britain will always be a democracy.

Whether Britain stays a democracy depends on which MPs get elected to run our country. That depends on how people vote in elections. And, very soon, that will include you.

Every nation is either a republic or a monarchy. A monarchy is a nation ruled by a monarch. A republic is a nation ruled by an elected representative, usually a president. Britain is a constitutional monarchy. This means that the monarch does not run the country: that is left to an elected government.

Job sheet

2 Please stay in pairs. Look at the stamps above. Which of these countries are monarchies and which are republics? Explain how you decided.

3 Even today, there are countries which are ruled by dictators. Your teacher may show you film about these countries. How are the citizens' lives affected by being ruled by a dictator?

2 Belonging to a community

KEY *words*

community councillor resident

Each of us is a citizen of a nation. But we belong to other communities as well. A community is simply a group of individuals who are linked in some way. A school is a community. So is a college. And so is the town or village in which you live.

People don't always choose their community. You may be at college because there's nowhere else to study the courses you have chosen. There are probably people living in your town who are there because that's where their job is. They might prefer to be somewhere else – but they are still members of the local community.

Many people are proud of their community; they want others to know that they belong to it. Your town probably has a crest which it puts on all official papers. It may even elect a mayor as its representative.

There are also many smaller communities which are made up of people who have chosen to join them. Churches are one example: Christians choose to go to church and be a member of a Christian community. This is just one religious community: there are plenty of others.

In fact, nearly everyone belongs to a number of communities. Each small community plays its part in helping a larger community.

Perhaps you've seen a sticker like this on a window. It's a sign that the owner belongs to a Neighbourhood Watch scheme. This means that residents try to keep an eye on each other's houses. If they notice anything unusual, they tell the police.

There would be few good things happening in your town or village without all the different communities. They run charity events; they take meals to old people and help couples whose marriages are in trouble. They organise outings for children and sick people.

Even in your school or college there are many communities. Your tutor group is one of them. So is your chess club (if you've got one) and the netball team. If they are good communities, people enjoy belonging to them – and they will benefit the whole school or college.

There are all sorts of ways to help your community. But first you have to make your views known. That is what Tessa Melling did.

A nine-year-old girl has won a breathing space for more than 50 trees facing the axe – by pleading for the squirrels nesting in their branches.

'What would you think if a giant squirrel came and chopped your house down?' Tessa Melling asked in a letter to her local council. 'What do you think all those squirrels are going to think when you chop down all the trees?'

Leicestershire County Council was ready to approve plans to chop down the trees to make way for a housing development when it received Tessa's letter.

But councillors were so touched by her 'save our squirrels' plea that they have now decided not to give the go-ahead until after further talks with residents and the local council.

A total of 53 trees, including yew, ash, hawthorn, pine, sycamore and an oak, were threatened by the scheme.

Councillor Phil Knowles said: 'I think everyone was taken aback by the letter.'

How to make your community more secure

By being a good neighbour, and keeping an eye out for anything suspicious you can help to make your community more secure. These are some of the things you should report:

- strangers knocking on front doors or peering through windows then disappearing round the back, or loitering suspiciously;
- strangers hanging round schools, playing fields, etc, and approaching children;
- open windows in houses where the owners are out or on holiday;
- strangers trying car doors;
- anything that *you* believe is suspicious.

DETAILS ARE IMPORTANT – Whenever you pass on information, remember that accurate descriptions of suspected people and vehicles, etc, will save time and confusion.

This is the information the police will need

- **an exact description of what you have seen;**
- **the time;**
- **the place;**
- **the person(s) involved: approximate age, sex, height, build, unusual characteristics, clothing worn, and any other distinguishing features;**
- **the vehicles involved: registration number (even part of this number might help), make and model (if known), colour and direction of travel.**

Crime prevention advice

Advice on all aspects of crime prevention is freely available from the Crime Prevention Officer at your local police station.

GOOD NEIGHBOURS – KEEP WATCH – CUT CRIME

F1 Prepared for the Home Office by the Central Office of Information 1985
Printed in the UK for HMSO Dd 8170265 HOME J1001RP 2/89

Job sheet

1 a) Which communities do you belong to?
b) Describe the part you play in each of them.
c) What benefits do you get from being a member of these communities?

2 a) Read the column opposite. What five things should Neighbourhood Watch members report?
b) Suggest how the community benefits from having the first four things reported.
c) What do you think would count as 'suspicious'?

3 a) Read the story above. Which *two* communities was Tessa helping? (*Think!*)
b) What else could she have done to stop the trees being chopped down?

4 a) Work in pairs. Imagine you could plan a Community Centre for your area. It must offer services to the whole community. Write down what it would offer.
b) Explain which smaller communities would benefit from the services you would provide.

3 Other communities

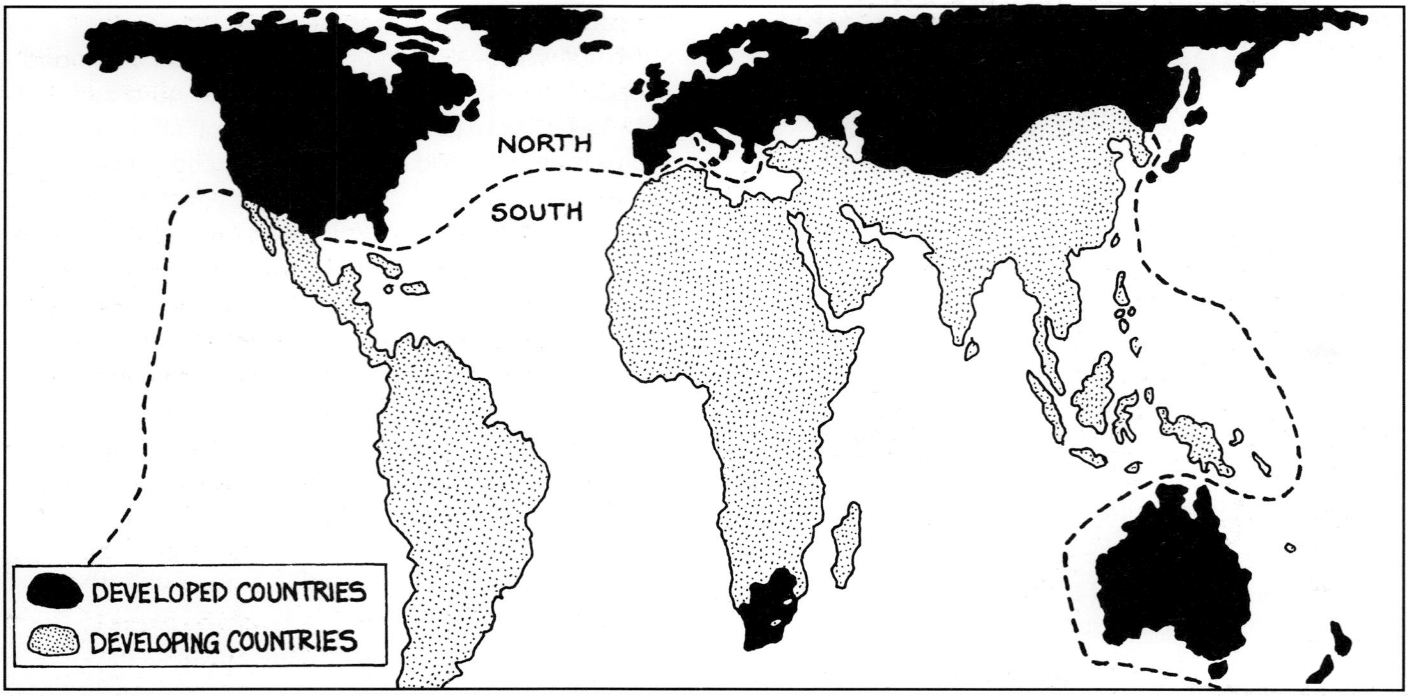

This map shows the size of countries more accurately than the world map you may be used to.

Each small community is part of a larger one. That is true of Britain, too. Britain is just one of the countries in the world. Each of us is a citizen of the world. So it is fair to ask: are we good citizens?

Look at the map above. It divides the world into two parts. One part contains all the richest countries; the other part contains the rest. Most of the well-off countries are in the north; in the southern hemisphere there is great poverty.

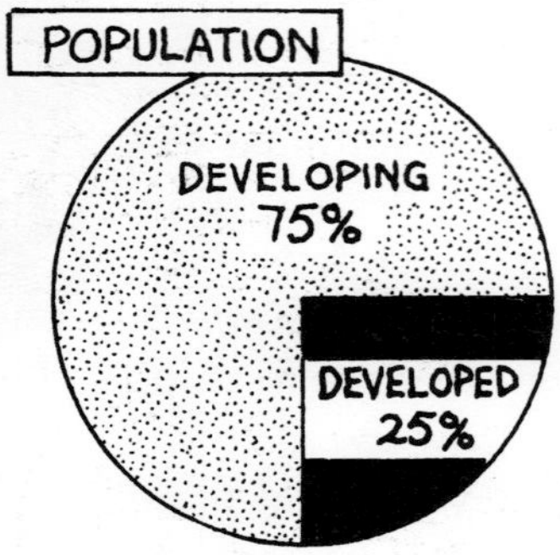

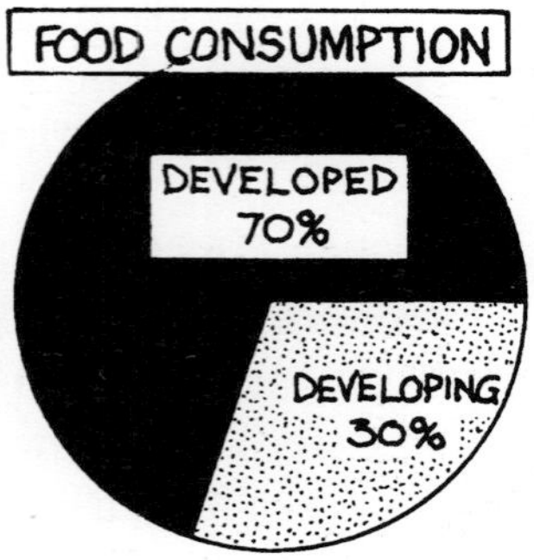

So we may be very lucky. We may happen to live in a developed country. We may have big industries. We can usually afford education and health care. On average, people living in developed countries earn *forty times* more than those living in developing ones.

KEY words

bilateral aid

Why does this matter? As long as we're okay, should we be worried about people elsewhere? One answer is that Britain cannot go it alone in the world, any more than any other country can.

Most of the poorer nations once belonged to someone's empire. Many of them were in the British Empire. These colonies helped make Britain rich in the 19th century. Although they're poor, they are still helping northern countries stay rich today.

The reason is trade. Every country must sell goods to earn money. So the poorer nations sell crops to the richer nations. They could grow richer by developing their own industries. But that costs money.

In the 1970s, developing nations borrowed a lot of money to build up their industry. Today, they are still paying back these debts. This means they have less to spend on improving their own health and education services.

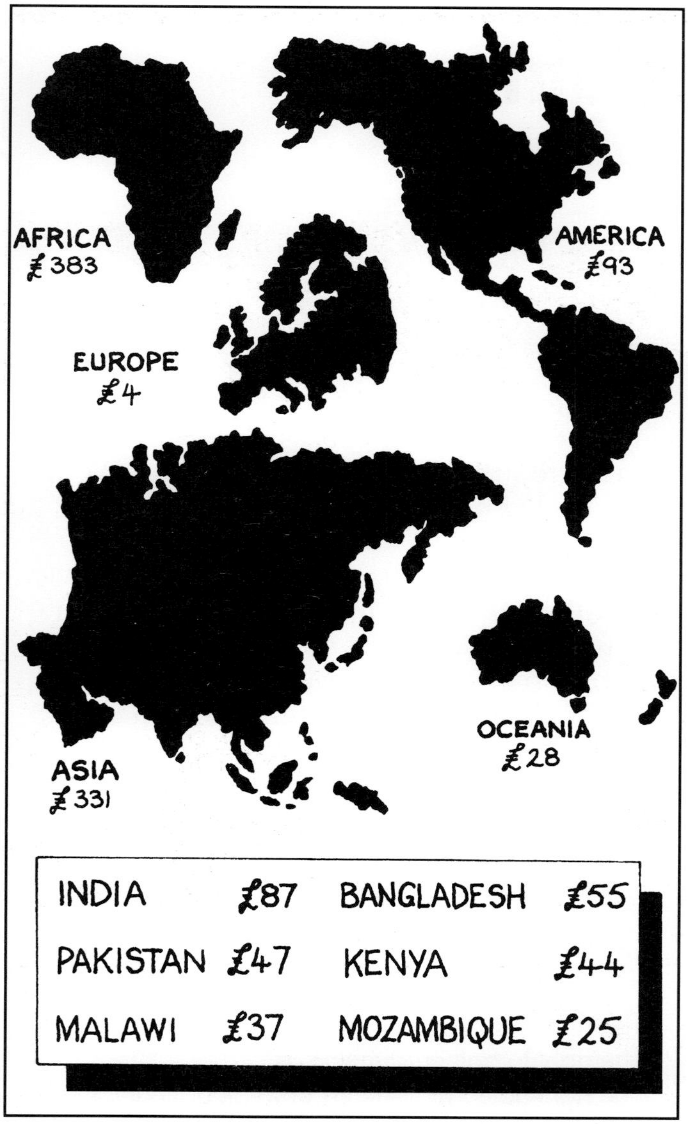

Where Britain's bilateral aid goes. Amounts shown are in millions of pounds.

Britain *does* help these poorer countries. In 1990, it spent over £1700 million on overseas aid. Much of this was given on one condition: the poorer country had to use it to buy British goods and services.

The rest of the money went to organisations, such as the United Nations, which help poorer countries. We gave the UN £113 million. It decides how to spend this money, although some of it is spent on British products.

Job sheet

1 a) You need an atlas for this question. Using the map opposite, write down the names of at least ten developed countries.
b) Write down the names of ten developing nations.

2 a) What do poorer countries need money for? Try to list at least ten things.
b) Now, put these things into order of importance. Be ready to explain how you decided.

3 a) Do you think Britain is right to expect other countries to spend aid on British goods? Give reasons.
b) Can you think of any disadvantages of this? Again, give reasons.

4 Please work in groups. Look at what the people below are saying. Discuss each statement. Only write down those with which you all agree. You should try to agree on at least two statements. Be ready to explain your choices to the class.

For and against – should Britain be helping more or is it a waste of time?

4 A British citizen's rights

Every person living in Britain has certain rights. Think about your school, for a start. Your parents had the right to choose which school you should go to. Once you got there, you had the right not to be beaten. You had the right to attend lessons and receive a proper education for free. On the other hand, the school had rights, too. It could exclude you if you broke its rules.

These rights are given to us by Parliament. Each right is written down in a law. We have the right to do anything which is not forbidden by law.

KEY words

Parliament

There are so many things that the law allows us to do that it would take books to list them all. The two picture strips show you some of them. We are so used to these rights that we take them for granted.

But our rights as citizens depend on where we live. Millions of people living in some African or South American countries do not have these rights. The police may arrest them and lock them up for weeks or months without putting them on trial. If they speak out against the government, they are arrested – or murdered.

Many people believe that all human beings should have the same rights, no matter where they live. Politicians in Europe even drew up a list of what they thought these rights should be. This is their list.

1 The right to say openly what you believe
2 The right to gather at meetings
3 The right not to be tortured or treated inhumanly
4 The right to live in private and as a family without interference
5 The right to be treated equally, whoever you are and whatever you believe

Some of our rights in Britain.

More rights in Britain.

It is a tradition that people may speak freely at Speaker's Corner in London's Hyde Park.

Perhaps it is easier to understand these rights if we imagine what life would be like without them. The next account has been made up: it tells the story of Sandy McKendrick; she lives in a Britain in which people have no rights. Which rights are missing?

Sandy's journey to school is never easy, although it is only half a mile away. The problem is that she lives on a Catholic estate; between her house and school lies a Jewish District and Catholics are not allowed to enter it.

So she goes to school by bus – a three-mile ride which her parents must pay for. When her dad is unemployed, she simply doesn't go to school.

On Mondays, she is quite happy not to go to school. She hates geography lessons because the teacher hits anyone who talks during the lesson. Once her dad went to school to complain about this but the headteacher called the police.

They arrived and took Sandy's dad away. 'You Catholics are all the same,' they told him. 'You're downright criminals.' And they locked him up. It was two weeks before they let him go. He wasn't charged with anything but they gave him a good beating before they let him out.

When he got home, he found his neighbours had ransacked the house; the TV and video had disappeared and the walls were daubed with slogans. 'You'd better call the police,' said his wife.

'No point,' said Mr McKendrick. 'They never do anything if a Catholic's house is attacked. You know that. It's been like that ever since the government stopped Catholics voting in elections.'

Job sheet

1 a) Please work in pairs. Read the story about Sandy's family. What rights do they not have that we have?
b) Write down the effects this has on their lives.
c) Which missing right do you think is most important? Be ready to present your ideas to the class.

2 Look at the list of rights on page 10. Who would suffer if these rights did not exist? Write down a different answer for each right.

3 a) Write down a set of rights for pupils. (Remember that rights must be for everyone.)
b) Write down a set of rights for teachers.
c) Compare the two lists. If there is a conflict, rewrite them.
d) Think carefully. Are you sure that the rights on your lists don't restrict someone else's rights?

5 The right to equal treatment

KEY *words*

prejudiced Briton minority discriminate stereotype

Over 57 million people live in Great Britain. Each of us is different in all sorts of ways. Yet we have the right to be treated equally. The 1976 Race Relations Act says so.

You cannot refuse to let people into a pub because of the colour of their skin or because they belong to a particular religion. You cannot refuse anyone a job for these reasons, either.

That's what the law says – but does it work out that way? Look at the graph below. It shows the percentage of people in each racial group who were unemployed in 1990. Study it very carefully.

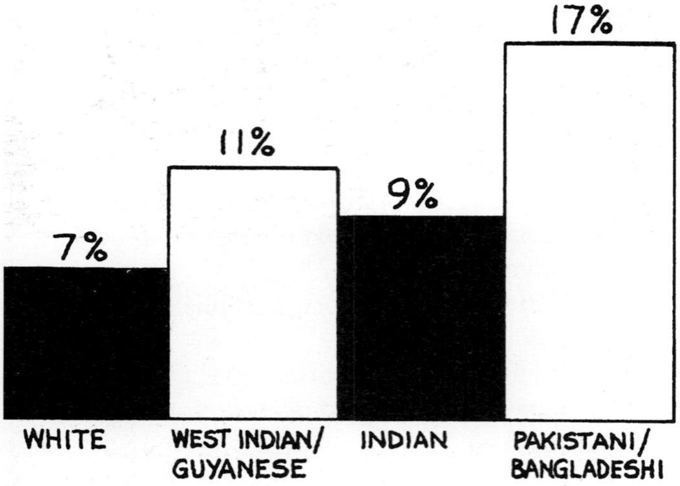

Job sheet

1 a) Put the groups in order, with the group with the lowest unemployment rate at the top.
b) Suggest as many reasons as you can for the differences between the groups.
c) Think carefully. Do these figures prove that people are treated equally or not? Explain how you decided.

What can we say about this man? Well, first, he's obviously prejudiced. He doesn't like foreigners but he doesn't give any good reason for not liking them. But, also, he's very confused. Not all white people are British – and not all Britons are white. In fact, even *white* Britons are a very mixed bunch indeed.

Britain was invaded a number of times after AD43 when the Romans landed. After the Romans came the Anglo-Saxons (from Germany) and the Vikings (from Scandinavia). Then, in 1066, there was an invasion by Normans. So even a white Briton is made up of quite a mixture of races.

As you can see, Britain has been a multi-racial society for centuries. The same is true of every country in Europe. This diagram shows the minority groups in the British population in 1989:

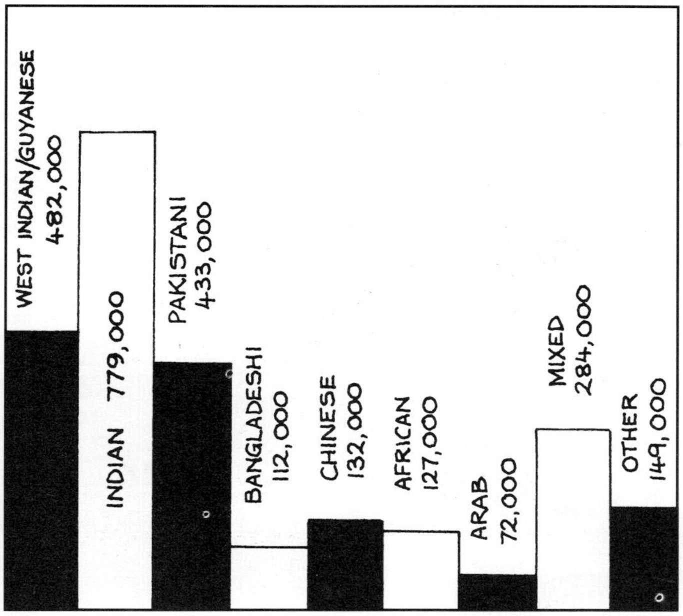

The law says that it is wrong to discriminate between people just on the basis of what race they belong to. Yet it still happens. You have probably done it yourself, without thinking about it. Look at this joke.

An Englishman, a Scotsman and an Irishman were travelling through the desert when their jeep broke down. Along came an Arab on a camel who offered to lead them to the nearest settlement. 'Bring what you need with you,' he told them.

The Scotsman took a bottle of Scotch. 'Why are you taking that?' asked the Arab.

'In case I get thirsty and need a drink,' said the Scot.

The Englishman took an umbrella. 'Why are you taking that?' asked the Arab.

'It's in case it gets too hot,' explained the Englishman. 'It will keep the sun off.'

The Irishman took the door off the jeep. 'Why are you taking that?' asked the Arab.

'Well,' said the Irishman, 'if it gets too hot, I can wind the window down.'

This joke is based on three stereotypes: the drink-loving Scotsman, the Englishman who always carries an umbrella and the stupid Irishman. These aren't real people: they are joke characters. It is ludicrous to think that a whole nation is stupid. Or, to put it another way, you can find stupid people in every nation.

For many years, it was the policy in South Africa that black and white people had to live separately. This policy was called *apartheid*. The white government passed laws to make sure that blacks and whites did not mix in public.

Naturally, each group had its own magazines and newspapers. The white newspapers had advertisements for suntan lotions which would help the white people to get darker skins. The black newspapers had advertisements for creams and lotions which would make black skins a lighter shade.

Manufacturers told black girls that they would be more likely to get a boyfriend if they bought tonics to straighten out their curly hair. Meanwhile, many white women went to beauty parlours to have their straight hair permed.

Job sheet

2 a) Please work in groups. On a single sheet of paper, write down things you have heard people say about other racial groups.
b) Go through the list, one by one. Where do you think they got these ideas from?
c) Which statements can you *prove* to be false? Be ready to present your findings to the class.

3 a) Read the column above. What were the white people doing?
b) What were the black people doing?
c) Why were the blacks and whites trying to do these things?
d) What is your opinion of their actions?

6 A citizen's duties

KEY *words*

slander libel damages perjury ombudsman

We hear a lot about rights these days. People are fond of pointing out that they have rights, if they're not getting their own way. But having 'a right to do something' isn't the same as saying, 'I have a right to do what I want.'

At the same time, people sometimes forget that they have duties, as well as rights. Most of our duties are laid down by law, just as our rights are. This means that we may be punished if we fail to do our duty.

For instance, it's our duty to respect other people's property. We cannot just walk into someone else's house without their permission. Even the police need a search warrant, unless they're actually pursuing a criminal or think a crime is happening.

In fact, every right implies a duty of some sort. On page 10, you saw that everyone has the freedom to say what they wish. It is our right. But it's not really quite as simple as that. We also have a duty to tell the truth. If we write or speak lies about someone, we may be punished.

The people who wrote these things were probably breaking two laws. First, they should not have defaced someone else's property; people have a right not to have their property damaged.

Second, if the things they wrote are not true, they have broken another law. If we write untrue things, we are guilty of libel. (If we speak lies about someone else, we are guilty of slander.) Suppose Anita is not pregnant. If she finds out who has written this, she can take them to court and demand damages for libel.

Every citizen has a duty to tell the truth. If, one day, you wind up in court as a witness, you will have to swear to tell 'the truth, the whole truth and nothing but the truth'. If you don't, you are guilty of perjury – and can be sent to prison.

In every aspect of life, we have duties. Can you add to these lists?

Sadly, not everyone does their duty at all times. So people need protection against those who break the law. That is why every nation has a police force. The police are there to make sure we carry out our duties – and to catch those who do not. Like everyone else, the police have a duty to tell the truth.

Sometimes, even officials can treat us unfairly. We need protection against that, too. So the government has appointed an ombudsman to deal with any complaints. If he or she thinks a person has been treated unfairly by officials, action can be taken to put it right.

But, in everyday life, there are lots of occasions when people do things because they *think* it is their duty – even though the law doesn't say it is. Most people think we have a duty to help the old, the sick and the young. There is no law which says that you must help an old person across the road but many people think we ought to do so.

We have a duty to look after our environment. People who drop litter can be fined. Claire Causton felt so strongly about it that she wrote to *Early Times*.

Recently we went to Alton Towers. We arrived early, before the crowds and the whole place was clean and tidy. Well, it was before the British public arrived. Waiting in the queue for the raging rapids, we spotted something unpleasant.

In front of us were a group of girls and one boy. They had obviously been given a packed lunch and threw various rolls and sweets into the boats going past. The boy was told that it was a silly thing to do and he asked why!

On the way back the people in front of us threw some rubbish out of their window. Since we were in a traffic jam, mum got out of the car, picked up the rubbish, walked up to their car and gave it back to them. They took it and then threw it out again.

Can't something be done or otherwise this country will earn itself a bad reputation.

Job sheet

1 Explain each of the key words.

2 a) Look at the citizen's duties in the picture above. For each one, suggest at least one reason why it is a duty.
b) Look at the parents' duties. Do you think parents have any *other* duties? Write down what they are and explain carefully why you think they are duties.

3 Look at this list of actions. Write down each one that you think is a duty and explain why you think so.
a) To hand in lost property.
b) To be polite to people.
c) To give up your seat on a bus to a pregnant woman.
d) To tell the truth at all times.
e) To rescue a drowning person.
f) To help around the house.

4 a) Read what Claire Causton wrote (above). Do you think we have a duty to keep Britain tidy? Give reasons.
b) Suggest how we could stop people dropping litter.

7 Helping other citizens

KEY words

moral duty **manifesto** **voluntary work**

There is no law that says you must help other people. The police will not arrest you for ignoring a drowning man. You won't appear in court for not stopping to help at a road accident. These are not legal duties.

Yet most people would say we have a moral duty to help others in need. In other words, we ought to do what we can for those who are less fortunate than ourselves. Every year, millions of people give money to charity for just this reason.

The government encourages this. Workers can give money to charity directly from their wages. The government gives tax relief on this; in other words, the worker pays no tax on the money he or she has given.

This is what one political party said about helping others in its 1992 election manifesto:

Charities and voluntary groups play a vital role in our national life. Britain is rich in its citizens' willingness to give time, effort and money to helping others. We have a great tradition of voluntary work at home and overseas. There are now about 350,000 voluntary groups in Britain – and personal donations to charities now amount to some £5,000 million a year.

Nicholas Killen, aged 6, had an operation to save his life. The operation made him blind in his right eye. He was already blind in the left one. The *Daily Mirror* reported:

Big sister Beverley hugged plucky Nicholas and pledged: 'I'll be your eyes.' Beverley, 18, promised to guide Nicholas as he returned to an emotional welcome from his six brothers and sisters.

She had already moved the furniture so that Nicholas could safely feel his way around.

Beverley explained: 'He will have to get used to the house without his sight. But until then, I'll guide him about and show him where things are.'

One school received this letter from a member of the public:

Sir,
This letter is several months overdue, to acknowledge the help received from various pupils of your school.

I am the man who frequently passes your school in a batricar vehicle. The original model was rather old and often broke down at awkward moments. During these emergencies, I often received help from your pupils.

Will you please publicly thank them for me. I do not know their names but please let them know I am very grateful.

Michele Elliott produced a report on bullying in schools in 1989. *Early Times* reported:

One of the conclusions in Michele Elliott's work was that most bullies are boys. Only a fifth of the reported bullies were girls. And most of them were at least a year older than their victims.

She found that 68 per cent of children complained of being bullied at some time. For 38 per cent, this had happened more than once, and was very frightening. More than two thirds of the victims were boys.

Michele goes around to schools talking to children about this. This is what she advises them to do:

- Tell an adult you trust;
- Tell yourself you don't deserve to be bullied;
- Get friends together and say 'No' to the bully;
- Stay with a group of people. There is safety in numbers;
- Try to ignore the bullying and try not to show you are upset;
- If you are different in some way, be proud of it. It's good to be an individual.

Job sheet

1 a) Write down a few examples of times when people outside your family have helped you.
b) For each case, suggest reasons why they did it.
c) How have you helped other people this term?
d) Write down the reasons why you helped them.
e) As a class, compare your reasons for helping other people.

2 Look at what the people on the left are saying. Which of these statements, if any, do you agree with?

3 a) What sort of help do you think you will need over the next 12 months?
b) Who do you think you will rely on to help you?

4 a) Please work in groups. Read the article above about bullying.
b) What can someone else do to help someone who is being bullied? Write all your ideas on a flipchart sheet.
c) Put your ideas in order of importance, with the best ideas at the top.
d) Discuss the class's ideas. Does anyone know of a younger child who's being bullied who can be helped now?

8 Family life

KEY words

nuclear family extended family surrogate

Most people first learn about the world from their family. Parents teach us what they think is right and wrong; they pass on any religious beliefs they may have. Long before we go to school, our family has helped to create the kind of person we will be.

For most people, their family plays a key role in their life, even long after they have left home. Yet each family is different. In most houses, just two generations of people live together – parents and children. This is called a nuclear family.

But in some houses, you'll find children and their parents living with other relatives, such as grandparents or aunts and uncles. We call this an extended family.

So when we talk about 'the family', each of us may have a different idea of what this means. For instance, most families have a legal basis. In other words, the parents are married. But a man and woman do not have to be married to have a family.

The picture below shows how a family usually looks in advertisements: two parents, two children and everyone's happy. Happy families help to sell goods – and this is an advertiser's idea of a happy family.

Of course, not all families are like this. Today, one in three British marriages ends in divorce. One child in three will find itself in a one-parent family before their sixteenth birthday.

As you would expect, one-parent families are usually much poorer than two-parent families. With two children, one parent needs up to 80% of the former joint income to keep up the same standard of living. Few one-parent families get as much money as this.

Like everything else in society, the family is changing. Medical progress means that women can now safely have children much later in life – up to their fifties. And it's possible for childless couples to have a baby from a surrogate mother.

It's even possible for an unmarried woman to have a baby by using sperm from a sperm bank. This means the child cannot have their real father around – and the child is unlikely ever to know who their father was.

Job sheet

1 a) Do a survey of your class. How many of you live in families like the one in the photograph on page 18?
b) Why, then, do advertisers show families like this?

2 a) In pairs, look at the photographs on this page. How is each family like or unlike your own?
b) Which of the families would you most like to be part of? Give reasons.
c) As a class, compare your answers to (b) and discuss any differences.

3 Are there any advantages or disadvantages in:
a) having a surrogate mother
b) being fathered from a sperm bank
c) having divorced parents
d) living with a step-parent?

4 How do you think a person's family background will affect what sort of citizen they become?

9 The family and tomorrow's citizen

KEY *words*

the state

There was a time when a family taught its children everything they needed to know. Today, many families rely on the state to do this for them. Some parents say, 'It's not my job to teach my children. Teachers are paid to do that.'

But it's not really that simple. Most children do not start school until they are four or five years old. Think of how much they have learnt in all that time.

The truth is that when we are little we learn almost everything from our family. Whatever parents may think, they don't leave teaching to schools. Everything a parent does is teaching a small child something – often when the parent doesn't intend it.

If you are not punished when you steal something, you grow up thinking it's all right to steal. If your parents are always shouting at each other, you assume that's normal behaviour. If they don't say 'please' and 'thank you', nor will you.

This, of course, can cause problems when the child goes to school. Schools punish pupils who steal. And children who always shout at other people soon find themselves in trouble. Schools have rules and expect pupils to follow them.

Job sheet

1 a) Write down any behaviour which is OK in your home but not in school.
b) Write down any behaviour in school which is not OK in your home.
c) As a class, compare your lists.
d) What do they tell you about how you have been educated at home?

In fact, parents have a duty to bring up their children in a way that will turn them into good citizens. Inevitably, that means making rules. It may also mean planning punishments if the rules are not obeyed.

And this is where families and the state are different. The state has laws which lay down what the punishment is for each crime. A judge cannot decide to hang someone for parking on double yellow lines: the law says how the person may be punished.

But no two families ever have exactly the same rules. No two sets of parents ever use exactly the same punishments. Some parents are strict; others are easy-going.

Family rules differ and so do the punishments.

13-YEAR-OLD BECOMES A MOTHER

Stephanie H— became a mother yesterday, just two days after her thirteenth birthday. Cuddling her son, Wayne, in hospital, she said: 'It's brilliant. I've always wanted to be a mum.'

The baby's father was not present at the birth. He attends the same school as Stephanie and was in his maths lesson at the time. The Headteacher refused to comment on the event.

But Stephanie's mother was only too willing to speak. 'I'm so sad for her,' she said. 'She's going to miss being a teenager, going out and enjoying herself.

'I blame the school. She should have been taught the facts of life but they don't start sex education until year 9. It's too late for Stephanie but other girls could be saved from a similar fate.'

WHAT PARENTS SAY

'I think rules are important. I would hate to think that my children were embarrassing other people or being naughty when they visited their friends. If they were really badly behaved, we'd never get baby-sitters and then we'd never go out. I certainly don't want my children showing me up.'

'Of course, children have to learn to behave themselves. When they're earning a living, they'll have to obey all sorts of rules. They can't suddenly learn how to behave when they start work. The process must start when they are little.'

'What they do at home is their concern, as long as they don't get under my feet. Schools have too many rules, if you ask me. I don't believe in them. In any case, our two know how to behave. They get a good thumping if they step out of line.'

Job sheet

2 a) Write down any rules you must follow at home.
b) For each one, say why you think it is a rule.
c) Which, if any, don't you agree with? Explain your answer.
d) Which of these rules do you think will help you when you leave home?

3 What might you learn about the adult world if:
a) your parents argue most of the time
b) nobody worries about what time you come home
c) your father drinks heavily
d) your parents are stricter with girls than boys
e) your parents don't say 'please' or 'thank you'?

4 In groups, discuss Stephanie's story. Is anybody to blame and, if so, who?

10 Leaving home

KEY ***words***

Income Support **contract** **tenant**

Nearly everybody says good-bye to their family sooner or later. It may happen when you go off to university or if you find a job in another town. Perhaps you cannot wait to leave home: the grass always seems greener on the other side of the fence.

But, needless to say, there are problems. First, you need somewhere to live. And the first thing you discover is that no one will guarantee this. Local councils must give you advice and help if you've got nowhere to live. But that's not the same as actually finding you a home.

Every big town and city has a long waiting list for housing. The teenager who simply leaves home is not a priority. Old people, handicapped people and those with children come first.

You probably won't get any government benefits, either. If you're under 18, you can get Income Support only under certain circumstances. You must be pregnant, suffer some sort of handicap or be at risk of sexual abuse if you stay at home.

A local council must provide some help to unemployed people who are living away from home. Usually, this means putting them in bed and breakfast accommodation. However, this only lasts for two or three weeks at the most. After that, you're on your own.

Of course, if you've got a job, you can afford to pay rent. And if you are on a training scheme away from home, accommodation should be provided. If someone has fixed up a flat for you, you're at an advantage. They should have checked for you that it's safe and clean.

If you're flat-hunting yourself, the job is not as easy as it sounds. Most landlords are not trying to cheat you but there is the odd exception. Making the right decision involves planning and quick thinking. Look at the job sheet to see if you could cope.

Job sheet

1 How would you decide if a flat is good value for money? Write down the things you would look for.
2 How would you decide if it was safe? List the points you'd look for.
3 How would you decide if it was a health hazard? Again, list what you'd look for.

When you rent a flat (or just a room), you make a legal agreement with the owner. This means you sign a contract which says what each of you must do and probably what you are allowed to do, too.

For instance, it may say that you cannot keep pets. If you break this contract, you may be told to leave. The same is true if you don't pay the rent. When you sign the contract, you're probably also agreeing not to damage the property or annoy the neighbours.

Is this the ideal tenant?

The contract lays down your duties. On the other hand, the law also gives you rights. For instance, if you pay rent weekly, you must be given a rent book. This states how much rent you pay and explains the terms of your agreement.

If you have any problems, you could go to a Citizens Advice Bureau to get advice. Or you could go to see the local rent officer. (The phone number will be in the phone book.) In some cases, he or she can actually decide whether your rent is fair or not.

But even this is not the end of your problems. The questions to ask yourself go on and on. Look at these, for a start:

- How much rent can you afford?
- How do you *decide* how much rent you can afford?
- Can you cope with being alone?
- Or can you cope with sharing a flat with other people?
- Do you have the skills to live on your own?

PERSONAL BUDGET SHEET

Net income
(after tax and national insurance) per week: £80

Rent 28.00

Fares to get to work 5.00

(Other expenses here) ....

....

....

....

....

....

DON'T LEAVE HOME, TEENAGERS WARNED

The Government is to spend a million pounds on a campaign aimed at warning teenagers about the dangers of leaving home.

Voluntary groups and police estimate at least 100,000 people are homeless in London.

The housing minister said part of the answer was to ensure 'that as many young people as possible stay close to their family home until they are sure of adequate alternative accommodation and have the financial means to support it'.

A report by the Salvation Army shows that almost 50,000 people sleep rough in central London every night. Another 50,000 squat in empty property or live in other unsuitable accommodation.

Job sheet

4 a) Copy out the budget sheet opposite.
b) List all the items you must spend money on each week.
c) Then, list the luxuries you'd like.
d) Write down the rough costs of each. The total must not exceed £80.
e) What are you missing, compared with living at home?

5 Which of these things have you ever done: (a) changed a plug; (b) mended a fuse; (c) used a launderette; (d) cleaned an oven; (e) used a public telephone; (f) dealt with cockroaches or mice; (g) cooked meat and vegetables; (h) used a bank or building society cash point; (h) dealt with a gas company which is threatening to take you to court?

6 Look at the things you have not done. How would you find out how to do them?

11 Our democracy

KEY *words*

democratic election elector

Once you have left home, you will make your own decisions. At home, with your family, you cannot make all the decisions on your own. There are other people to consider.

But, as we know, families differ. In your family, are the decisions shared by everyone? Can you all chip in with your ideas and agree on what to do? If so, your family is democratic. Or does your mum or your dad decide everything, without consulting anyone else? In that case, you're living with a dictator!

Job sheet

1 a) List the decisions your mother takes.
b) List the decisions your father takes.
c) List the decisions you share.
d) Do you think your family is democratic? Explain your answer.

In this way, countries are similar to families. Some try to share out the decisions and be democratic. Others are ruled by one person who makes all the decisions. These countries are known as dictatorships.

Countries run by a dictator may still allow people to vote but there's usually only one political party. So voters do not have any real choice. In some such countries, it is illegal not to vote – so people *have* to vote for the government.

However, Britain is a democracy. This means that most adults over the age of 18 share in making decisions. They do this by voting in elections. Electors vote for people who will represent them as Members of Parliament (MPs). MPs meet in the Palace of Westminster in London.

The Palace of Westminster.

Usually, the political party that has most MPs will form a government. The government then rules the country for up to five years. Each time it wants to make a new law, the MPs vote on the issue. Other issues may be decided locally by a local council which can make bye-laws. Once again, the councillors are chosen at elections.

The right to vote is very important. It's our main way of having a say in how the country is run. Yet not everybody exercises their right to vote. In the 1992 election, over 20% of people did not vote. Some people say they can't be bothered to vote because they're not interested in politics.

DEREK SPICER
Aged 15, Derek is captain of the football team and plays in the school band. He is of about average ability in lessons but good at nearly everything else he does. Derek is rather shy and rarely stands up for himself. He wants the council to have more power. Hobbies: football and music.

MARY McTAVISH
Aged 15, Mary has only been at the school for four months. She is more popular with the boys than with the girls. She is of below average ability. Her favourite subject is drama and she is rehearsing for the next school play. She does not have any plans for the council: she just feels she should be helping.

JOANNE BRUNE
Aged 14, Joanne is very popular with other pupils, both male and female, and with teachers. She is clever and outgoing but takes no part in out-of-school activities. She is concerned about litter in the school and with bullying. Her parents are very rich. Hobbies: horse-riding and foreign travel.

BHUPINDER PATEL
Aged 13, Bhupinder is a bit of a loner. His main concern is doing well at school and he works hard at everything he does. He is a very able pupil. He thinks the school council should be run only by pupils and that teachers should have nothing to do with it. He lives with foster parents.

It's time to elect a representative to the school council. Which one will you choose? (See question 4.)

Job sheet

2 a) What is the difference between a democracy and a dictatorship?
b) Why is Britain called a democracy?
3 Look at the cartoon on page 24. Do you think Sharon is right? Give reasons.
4 a) In groups, look at the four candidates shown above. Which information is *irrelevant* in making your choice?
b) You may only elect one pupil. Write down their name and your reasons for choosing that person.
c) Explain why you rejected the others.
d) Were any of them *ideal* candidates? Explain your answer.
e) As a class, discuss your answers. What can you learn from this about the difficulties of voting in an election?

12 Inside Parliament

KEY words

constituency bill constituent Mace

On election day, the polling stations close at 10 pm and the ballot boxes are taken off to a large building, such as a town hall. Rows of people then count all the votes. The candidate with the most votes becomes the new MP for the constituency.

Shortly afterwards, he or she will set off for Westminster in London to take their seat in the House of Commons. In fact, there are only 437 seats in the House and there are 651 MPs, so they can't all sit down at once. The drawing opposite shows what the House looks like.

Anyone can go and watch debates from the Visitors' Gallery. People sometimes queue to get a seat for major debates. There is another gallery for reporters (1) and one for the people who make an official record of what MPs say (2).

By tradition, the government sits on the left-hand side (3). Government ministers sit on the front bench. The party with the second highest number of MPs sits opposite them (4). They are known as the Opposition.

This person keeps the MPs under control. She is the Speaker (5). Her job is to keep order and make sure that MPs are not rude to each other. If things get too noisy, she shouts out, 'Order!' If this doesn't do the trick, she suspends the sitting so that everyone cools off.

At the end of a debate, the MPs vote. They walk out through the doors at the back (6). If they agree with what is being suggested, they walk through the Aye Lobby. If they disagree, they walk through the No Lobby. A division bell is rung when a vote is going to take place: MPs have just 8 minutes to get to the House and vote.

You may wonder why they're not all there already. The answer is that MPs don't just discuss things and vote. In the mornings, when there's no meeting in the House, they may attend a committee discussing some other bill.

There will be people to meet, too. Perhaps some of their constituents have come to London to ask for help. Or the MP might have agreed to do a TV interview. On top of that, there are letters to answer.

Job sheet

1 You need to watch a video of the House of Commons in session.

a) Does anything surprise you about how debates take place?

b) What do you think is the effect of having the two sides directly facing each other?

c) Is it important to know how our Parliament works – or doesn't it matter? Discuss your reasons.

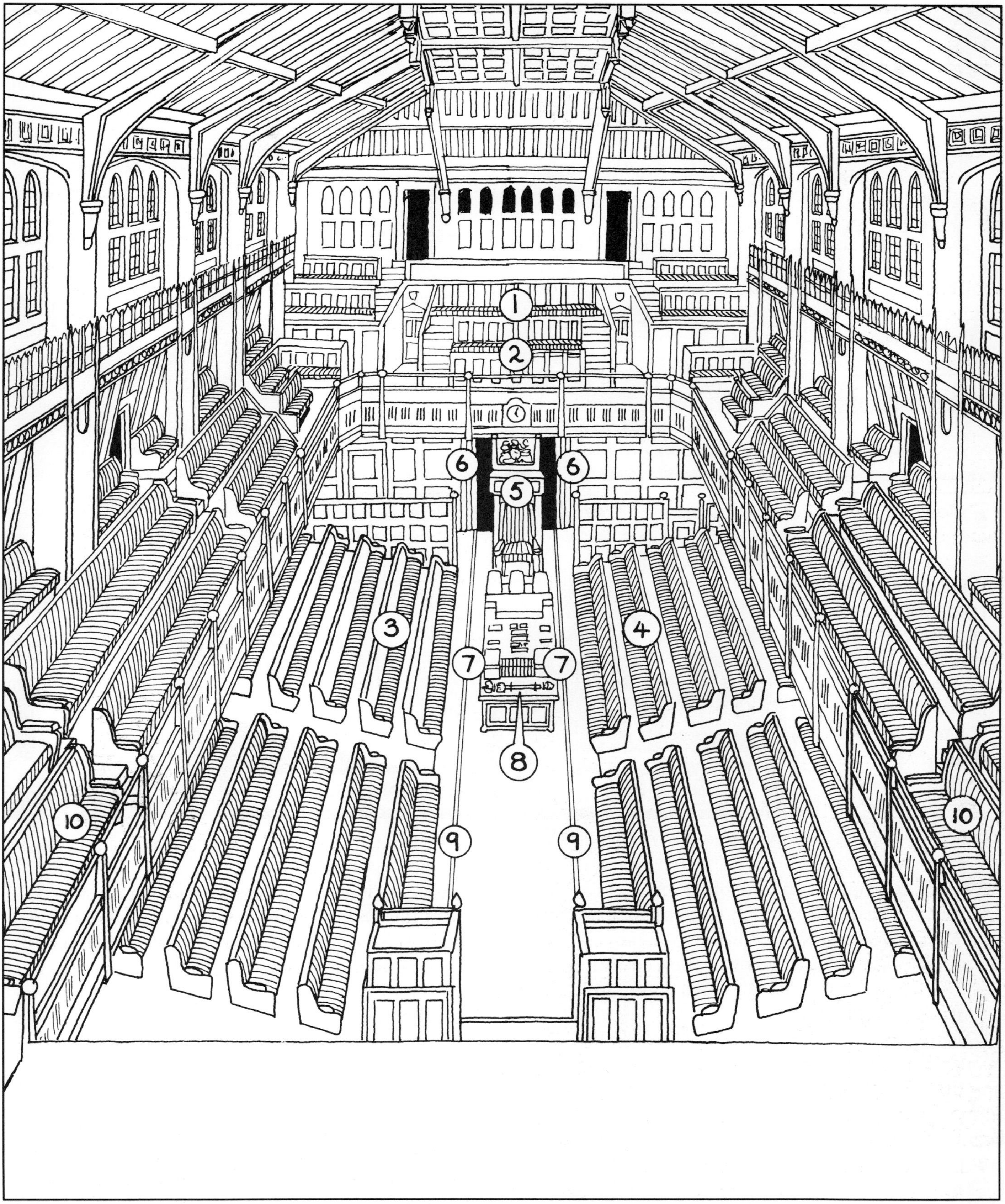

Inside the House of Commons. Places numbered 1–6 are mentioned on page 26. The other places are: 7 – despatch boxes where ministers and shadow ministers speak; 8 – the place where the Mace is put; 9 – the sword lines (MPs may not cross these while speaking); 10 – the Visitors' Gallery.

⑬ How democratic is Britain?

How a bill becomes law. The bill may be changed at stages 3, 4, 5 and 6.

Most adults over 18 can vote but a few cannot. Long-term prisoners and people in mental asylums are not allowed a vote. Nor is the monarch or members of the House of Lords; they have no vote because they already play a part in running the country.

The drawings above show how they do this. Members of the House of Lords can vote against any bill which they disagree with. In theory, the monarch can refuse to sign an Act of Parliament – but it would be very unlikely. It has become a tradition that she signs automatically.

This long process makes sure that each new law is discussed very carefully. But how democratic is this system? Voters can, of course, choose their MPs – but they do not elect members of the House of Lords. Nor is the monarch elected.

And there is another issue which many voters do not understand. When they vote, they vote for a man or woman to become their representative. But most candidates belong to a political party. Once they become MPs, the party has more control over them than the electors do.

Of course, if electors feel they have picked the wrong person, they can vote for someone else at the next election. But until then they have little control over what an MP says or does.

The party, though, has very great control. On many issues, the party will tell the MP how to vote. Party officials called 'whips' have the job of making sure their members vote – and vote in the way their party wishes. If an MP ignores the whips too often, he or she will never get promoted.

KEY ***words***

tradition conscience General Election

On a few issues, the parties will let MPs decide for themselves how to vote. These are usually moral issues, such as whether the death penalty should be re-introduced. Others include whether fox hunting should be banned and whether to change laws on abortion.

Some MPs listen to their constituents' views before they decide how to vote on these issues. But most of them vote according to their own conscience – in other words, they decide for themselves what is right and wrong. In recent years, they have decided that fox hunting is not wrong and that there should be no death penalty.

Some people think there is one other way in which Britain's voting system is not democratic. Our system is often called the 'first past the post' system. This means that, in each constituency, the candidate with the most votes becomes MP.

Why should anyone think this is unfair?

The answer lies in statistics. Look at these figures from the 1992 General Election. They show how many MPs each party had elected.

As you can see, the Conservative Party was the clear winner in terms of seats in Parliament. But, if you look at who people voted for, you get a rather different picture.

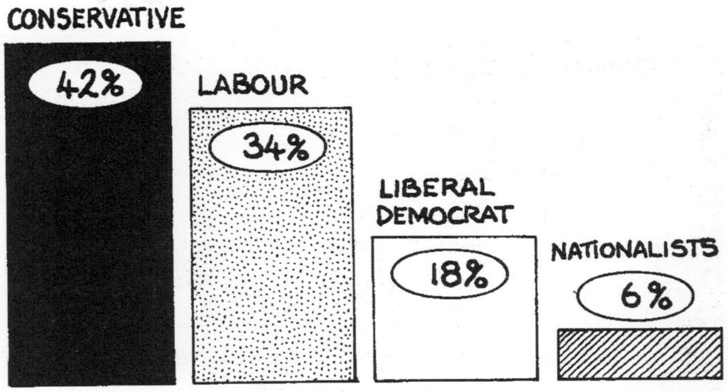

Some people think this is unfair. They would prefer Britain to have a voting system called Proportional Representation or PR. There are various kinds of PR system and most European countries use one sort or another.

With a PR system, the number of MPs elected depends on how many votes each party gets. Using one PR system, this is what the House of Commons would have looked like after 1992:

Conservative 272 MPs
Labour 223 MPs
Liberal Democrat 116 MPs

As you can imagine, the Liberal Democrats are keen on having a PR system. The Conservative Party and most of the Labour Party are not. Only Parliament can change the voting system. Is it likely that the winning party will end the system which has brought it to power?

Job sheet

1 a) What control do electors have over their MPs?
b) What control does a political party have over its MPs?
c) Who do you think has more control – electors or the political party? Give reasons.

2 Please discuss these questions in groups and try to reach an agreement.
a) Does it matter that the House of Lords is not elected?
b) Does it matter that the monarch is not elected?
c) Do you think the British political system is democratic?

14 Pressure groups

KEY *words*

lobby

Some people are not prepared to wait until another General Election before having their say in politics. These people feel so strongly about something that they try to make the government take action. We call them pressure groups.

A pressure group is one which tries to get action on a particular issue. Some are quite small, such as a local group trying to stop a by-pass. Others are big international organisations, such as Friends of the Earth.

There are other differences between pressure groups. Some are trying to protect their own interests. Trade unions, for instance, are pressure groups, working to get a better deal for their members.

In turn, most unions belong to the TUC (Trades Union Congress) – a pressure group which tries to protect the unions themselves. In the same way, industrialists have banded together in the CBI (Confederation of British Industry). They aim to get governments to listen to industry's needs.

But perhaps the best-known pressure groups are those which promote a special cause. Their members are often very committed to the cause and will work very hard to get publicity for it.

There are all sorts of ways they can get this publicity. Some of them are illustrated below. As you can see, some techniques will get more publicity than others. Occasionally, pressure group members might even try illegal methods.

Sometimes, two pressure groups aim to achieve the same thing but in different ways. For instance, the RSPCA tries to stop cruelty to animals. It prosecutes people who break the law and it gets publicity on TV and in newspapers.

At the same time, a group called the Animal Action Group has taken its own actions. It wants to stop animals being used in laboratory experiments. Some of its members have broken into laboratories and taken film of how animals are used. They have even released animals.

There is one other thing which a pressure group can do. It can pay an MP to act as its consultant. What this means is that the MP will try to represent the views of the pressure group.

An MP can do this by trying to persuade other MPs to support the group's aims. One pressure group which pays MPs to be consultants is the tobacco industry. It hopes that, in return, the MPs will persuade the government not to take action which might harm the tobacco companies, such as putting up the tax on cigarettes.

But the tobacco companies don't have it all their own way. There are also two pressure groups which try to stop people smoking. The biggest is Action on Smoking and Health (ASH). One of its campaigns aims to stop tobacco companies from advertising.

The other group is called PaT (Parents Against Tobacco). In 1990, when PaT was started up, *Early Times* printed this report.

PaT wants to see fines of up to £10,000 for selling cigarettes to children, among other strict measures. PaT wants to see a law that forces local authorities to act against shops breaking the Protection of Children Act.

And if they do there won't be a lack of cases. PaT groups throughout the country checked out which of their local shops would sell to children. The total result, nationwide, was that 224 out of 418 did – over 50 per cent.

Further to that, they want a complete ban on tobacco adverts on shop fronts and at points of sale and a limit on TV coverage of sports events sponsored by tobacco firms.

Job sheet

1 Please work in groups with large sheets of paper. Read the news item above and look at the cartoons on page 30. Devise a publicity campaign for PaT. (It must not be expensive.)
   a) Decide four actions you can take.
   b) Put them in the order in which you will carry them out.
   c) For each one, write down your aim.
   d) Now, think hard about your chances of success. Write down any reasons why your campaign may not work.

2 a) As a class, discuss your conclusions.
   b) Do you think a pressure group is ever justified in breaking the law?

3 a) Write to a pressure group of your choice, inviting a representative to come and talk to you.
   b) Plan some questions to ask about their aims, methods and the results they have achieved.

15 European citizens

It is not only the British Parliament which affects our lives. These days, all countries depend on each other. Britain was a founder member of the United Nations (UN) when it was set up in 1945. If a war breaks out, Britain is ready to send soldiers for a UN peace-keeping force.

Since 1969, Britain has also been a member of the European Economic Community. It now calls itself the European Community (EC). Its total population is greater than that of the United States. This map shows who belongs to the EC.

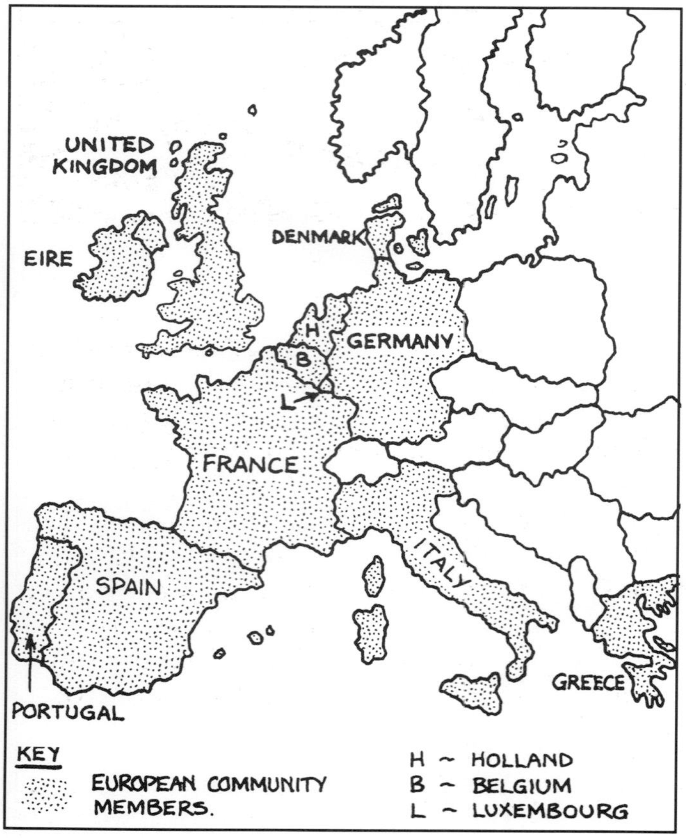

What does being a member of the EC mean? Does it really mean anything in our daily lives? After all, our government makes laws in London. What's the EC got to do with us?

The answer is: quite a lot. The EC, too, makes laws which affect our lives. Like any club, the EC has rules. Each country which joins has to accept them. These rules are written down in the Treaty of Rome. When Britain joined, it had to sign this treaty. So we, too, have to obey the EC's rules.

KEY *words*

EC **institution** **civil servant**

WHO RUNS THE EC?

The EC has its own Parliament which meets at Strasbourg in France. Each member country elects its own Members of the European Parliament (MEPs). The UK has 81 MEPs, elected by the 'first past the post' system. The European Parliament discusses new policies but it cannot make new laws. This photograph shows it in action.

Decisions are actually made by the Council of Ministers. This has twelve members, one from each EC country. This is the most important institution in the EC.

However, even this group does not come up with ideas for new policies. That is left to the European Commission. This has seventeen officials. They are not elected; instead, the government of each country chooses one or two members. This Commission also makes sure that new policies are carried out. It controls the 6000 civil servants who actually run the EC.

Finally, the European Court of Justice settles any arguments between countries. It decides whether any member country is breaking EC law and makes sure that EC laws are obeyed.

Just a few of the ways in which being an EC member has affected us.

Perhaps this all sounds very remote. What does it mean in practice? Has being an EC member helped us? As you might expect, people do not agree about this. Some people think we must stay in the EC because our economy would be far worse if we were outside it.

Others think being a member has been a disadvantage and we ought to get out as quickly as possible. Even politicians cannot agree about it. In both the Labour and Conservative parties there are MPs who think we should stay in; there are also a few MPs in both parties who want us to get out.

It is unlikely now that Britain will leave the EC. In your lifetime, the EC will probably make even more new laws which will affect not only you but your children and grandchildren. We may not be aware of it but the EC is part of our lives.

Quite how it will develop is anyone's guess. The EC is a family of nations and, like any family, it has its arguments. But these are tiny compared with the great arguments in Europe earlier this century which led to two world wars. The EC exists partly to stop that happening again. For that reason, we should all hope that it works.

Job sheet

1 Read the second column on page 32. Explain what each of these does:
   a) the European Parliament;
   b) the Council of Ministers;
   c) the European Commission;
   d) the European Court of Justice.

2 a) How can an ordinary person affect what the EC does? Please answer carefully.
   b) How democratic do you think the EC is? Give reasons.

3 a) Look at the picture strip above. Which of the six pictures show a benefit to Britain?
   b) In each case, say who benefits.
   c) What disadvantages can you see?

4 Which do you think is more important – being a good British citizen or being a good European? Please answer in detail.

16 The citizen and the law

Steps towards appearing in court.

KEY *words*

enforcing **remanded in custody** **bail** **juvenile**

For every right you have, someone else has a responsibility. You have a *right* to walk down the street without being attacked: that means that other people have a *responsibility* to leave you in peace.

However, there are always some people who don't want to follow the rules. Society must take action to make sure that people like that are dealt with. So Britain has laws which we all must follow. The police have the job of enforcing these laws. They *don't* make the laws and they *don't* decide who is guilty or innocent. Politicians make the laws and courts decide who is guilty.

In fact, there are actually two kinds of law – and the police usually only deal with one of them. They are concerned with *criminal* law – and their first task is to *prevent* crimes happening. But it is impossible to stop every crime from taking place. So their other job is to find out who has committed crimes and take them to court. The pictures above show the steps they go through.

It may take months before a case actually comes to court. The police have to gather evidence to prove their case. At the same time, the accused person may also gather evidence to show that they are innocent.

An accused person is entitled to have a solicitor represent him or her in court. If the accused has no money, this help will be provided free. The solicitor helps the accused person to get a defence organised.

Eventually, the case will be heard in a Magistrates' Court. A panel of magistrates listens to the evidence; afterwards, they decide if the accused is guilty – and how they should be punished. There is no jury in this type of court.

Most criminal cases are settled in a Magistrates' Court. Cases involving serious crimes such as murder are passed on to Crown Courts. In these courts, a jury decides if the person is guilty and a judge decides what the sentence shall be.

There is another branch of the law called *civil* law. This is concerned with disagreements between individuals. For instance, if a builder makes a mess of your extension, you may want compensation. You could take action against the builder under civil law. Cases where you accuse someone of slander or libel are also civil law matters.

An accused person's rights.

Job sheet

1 Put these events into the correct order:
   a) a suspect is cautioned;
   b) a suspect is arrested;
   c) a crime is committed;
   d) a suspect is released on bail;
   e) a suspect is charged.

2 a) What part do each of these play in the legal process: (i) the police; (ii) magistrates; (iii) politicians?
   b) What is (i) civil law and (ii) criminal law?

3 What effects would it have if:
   a) the accused person was guilty until proved innocent;
   b) the accused person wasn't allowed to give evidence;
   c) a person could be found guilty, even if there were doubts;
   d) juvenile cases were heard in public?

17 It's for you to judge

Politicians decide how people who commit a crime may be punished. Magistrates and judges decide exactly what punishment to give in a particular case.

There are so many kinds of crime that only people in the legal profession know them all. In fact, it will really help to have a police officer with you for this lesson. The rest of us know that it's wrong to kill someone or steal their property. But how many other crimes do you know about?

Job sheet

1 List all the other crimes you know about.
2 Now, list the possible punishments for each one.

The chances are you did not get very far, especially with question 2. For instance, it's illegal to drive a car with tyres with less than 1.6mm of tread left on them. The maximum punishment is a fine, but courts do not have to fine someone found guilty.

Job sheet

3 Look at the picture strip opposite. Write down each number on a separate line in your book. Beside it, write CRIME if you think a crime has been committed or NO CRIME if you think none has.
4 a) Compare your answers to question 3 with other people in the class. Are there any you can't agree about?
b) Now, ask the police officer to tell you what's illegal and what isn't.
c) Do any of the cases surprise you?

ARE THESE CRIMES OR NOT ?

You're also going to need the police officer's help with the remaining questions. This page contains three case histories. In each one, at least one crime has been committed. Your job is to work out what the crimes were – and decide what punishment you would give in each case.

The law changes often. At the same time, the government is always looking for new ways to deal with criminals. Even if someone is found guilty, magistrates and judges usually have a number of ways in which they can punish the offender. And these punishments change from time to time. Your officer can tell you what the possible punishments are at the moment.

CASE 1

James Raynor, aged 12, broke a window in a neighbour's house by throwing a stone at it. When the police came round, he denied that it happened and his parents said he was out shopping with them at the time. But they knew James had done this sort of thing before and the stone had his fingerprints on it.

CASE 2

Wayne Rapson, aged 16, lives with his parents in a block of council flats. He's keen on heavy metal and plays tapes until late into the night. The neighbours have complained to his parents and the police have been round to warn him on several occasions.

Mr Peters, who lives next door, has a sick elderly mother. Wayne's noise keeps her awake at night. When the police fail to stop the noise, Mr Peters takes action into his own hands. He walks into the Rapsons' flat through an open door and smashes up Wayne's cassette player.

CASE 3

Shirley has a part-time job at the corner shop, which she began when she was 13. Now aged 15, she works on Saturdays and Sunday mornings, as well as three hours a day after school. The money came in useful but, as she got older, she always seemed to need more cash than she'd got.

Often, Shirley was alone in the shop. Her friend Cheryl (also aged 15) suggested that she should come in and take a few things while Shirley turned the other way. They agreed to split the proceeds.

For two months, their plan succeeded until a friend's mother caught her daughter Abby with a packet of expensive cigarettes – and the story came out. On this occasion, Shirley had sold the cigarettes to Abby. The police knew nothing about Cheryl's involvement. Shirley lost her job and the shop owner employed Cheryl instead.

Job sheet

5 a) Please work in groups. Decide what crimes (if any) have been committed by the young people in each case.

b) The police officer will tell you what punishments are available to you. You decide what punishments to give.

c) Decide what crimes the adults have committed.

d) As a class, compare each group's answers to (b). Discuss any differences.

e) The officer can tell you what crimes the adults have committed and how they might be punished.

⓲ Do you know your rights?

The law restricts young people's rights in their own interests. No one would seriously want 5-year-olds to go to prison or 8-year-olds to fight for their country. Nor does society want infants becoming drug addicts or very young children having to work for long hours.

It is not the same everywhere in the world. Many young children work long hours every week. Either they don't have the right to an education or their parents need them to go to work to bring in money. So what is illegal in Britain may well be allowed in other countries.

Marriage is a good example. In Britain, you cannot marry until you are 16 – and then only with your parents' permission. But in some other countries (including parts of the United States), you may marry at age 13 (or even younger).

In Israel, most Jewish men over 18 have to do military service. So do unmarried Jewish women.

But Britain's marrying age is not fixed for all time. The job of governments is to change laws if they feel that circumstances have changed. Until 1969, you had to be aged 21 to vote in an election. But politicians believed that young people were becoming more mature. So they brought the voting age down to 18.

People disagree about laws which give us rights. Even judges sometimes think that the law is wrong, as in this case.

An Old Bailey judge lashed out yesterday at laws which stop him locking up a dangerous 13-year-old boy.

The youngster, helped by two young men, kidnapped a 14-year-old, beat him unconscious, burned his chest with a cigarette and carved his initials on the victim's back. The terrified youngster was dumped outside his school gates.

Judge Bruce Laughland QC, sentenced the 13 year old to three months' detention last week. But yesterday the furious judge was forced to scrap the sentence after a lawyer told him it was illegal to cage anyone under 14 unless they are killers.

Judge Laughland warned it would not be his fault if the boy committed more serious crimes. He said, 'Parliament has deprived the courts of detention power of a person of this age for this grave crime.'

The judge was forced to put the boy under a supervision order.

Job sheet

1 Look at the list of rights on this page. For each right (list the numbers only), write down the age at which you think you can do it.
2 Invite a local police officer along to tell you how many you got right.

1 You can sell goods in the street.
2 You can buy fireworks.
3 You can vote.
4 You can buy a pet.
5 You can do a part-time job.
6 You can have your own bank account.
7 You can be convicted of a crime (if it can be proved you know the difference between right and wrong).
8 You can watch a U certificate film.
9 You can go into a pub.
10 You can buy alcohol in a pub.
11 You can drink alcohol with a meal in a pub.
12 You can sell scrap metal.
13 You can buy cigarettes.
14 You can take money out of a savings account.

15 You can be held fully responsible for a crime.
16 You can be fingerprinted.
17 You can leave school.
18 You can adopt a child.
19 You can buy on hire purchase.
20 You can pawn an object in a pawn shop.
21 You can join a trade union.
22 You can get married with your parents' permission.
23 You can get married without your parents' permission.
24 You can sit on a jury.
25 You can get a passport.
26 You can leave home with your parents' permission.
27 You can leave home without your parents' permission.
28 You can appear in an adult court.
29 You can be sent to prison to await trial (boys only).
30 You can be sent to prison to await trial (girls only).
31 You can be convicted of a sexual offence (boys only).
32 You can be convicted of a sexual offence (girls only).
33 You can own a house.

34 You can take out a mortgage.
35 You can go abroad as an entertainer.
36 You can drive a 125cc motorbike.
37 You can drive a car on a public road.
38 You can change your name.
39 You can hold a moped licence.
40 You can claim Social Security benefit.
41 You can make a will.
42 You can be a candidate in an election.
43 You can buy premium bonds.
44 You can choose your own doctor.
45 You can sell alcohol.
46 You can be sent to Borstal.
47 You can have sexual intercourse (girls only).
48 You can buy alcohol.

Job sheet

3 When you know the answers you may discuss:
a) which ones most surprised you and
b) which, if any, you disagree with. (Be ready to give your reasons.)

19 Your leisure and others' rights

KEY *words*

anti-social

Our leisure time is increasing all the time. Surveys show that women who do full-time jobs have an average of 37 hours' free time each week. Men have even more – over 46 hours each week.

On top of that, holidays are getting longer. Over 90% of manual workers get four or more weeks' paid holiday. Nearly 30% of all workers get five weeks or more.

We can add to that two other facts. First, many people are retiring at a younger age than in the past. Second, many people will face at least one period of unemployment in their lives.

It all adds up to a lot of leisure time. How do we use it? According to one survey, this is how young people aged 15 to 24 spent their time:

Men	%	*Women*	%
Pub	52	Dancing	54
Pop music	50	Going out with partner	53
Playing sports	48	Parties	50
Going out with partner	47	Friends	50
Friends	43	Pop music	47
Parties	43	Shopping	38
Dancing	38	Pub	38
Attending sports	35	Reading	35
TV	30	TV	35
Cinema	27	Walks	34
Reading	25	Radio	31
Radio	22	Playing sports	28
Walks	20	Cinema	26
Theatre/concerts	16	Theatre/concerts	19
Cards	13	Attending sports	18
Classical music	11	Cards	11
Shopping	6	Classical music	10
Church	4	Church	6

Job sheet

1 a) Make a class survey of time spent on leisure activities. Put the results in order, with the most popular at the top.
b) How do they differ from the results shown on the left?
c) In the last week, how much of your leisure time has been spent helping others?
d) In the last week, how much of your time has been spent in anti-social activities?

At first sight, leisure has got nothing to do with citizenship. After all, does it affect other people if a couple like to spend their free time down at the pub?

The answer is that it might do. Suppose that they like to go drinking *every* night – but they don't have the money to pay for a baby-sitter for their young children. So they're left alone in the house.

Or suppose that the parents' idea of a good evening out is to get as drunk as possible.

In fact, whether people drink alcohol at all affects every taxpayer in Britain. The government relies on getting income from taxes on alcohol. If everyone drank less, the government would have to look for other ways to get money. Income tax might have to go up.

So how we enjoy ourselves *does* affect other people. The key question is: *how much* does it affect other people? Does our way of having fun spoil life for someone else?

Job sheet

2 a) Look at the picture above. Which people are doing something which spoils someone else's enjoyment?
b) Discuss whose interests should take priority.
c) How would you settle disagreements about this?

These are not just problems for individuals to sort out. They affect all of us. Sometimes they involve the police. Sometimes they involve the government.

Even your local council has to make decisions about leisure. It must decide how to spend its money: will your town get a better swimming pool or should they put more money into helping the local theatre? Does the town need new tennis courts or should the council put on more entertainment for young people?

Each of us has our own views about this. Each of us would like the council to cater for our own interests. The council's job is to weigh up the conflicting demands and decide which of them it should support. It cannot afford all of them – and we cannot all have our own way.

20 Citizens at work

KEY *words*

voluntary organisation

When people talk about working, we usually think of going out to do a job and getting paid for doing it. But there are plenty of kinds of work that don't fit this pattern.

For a start, you don't have to go out to earn a living. It is possible to do a paid job at home. Many writers work at home; so do cartoonists, artists and composers. You don't need to go to an office to write pop songs.

Working at home is becoming more common. It can be cheaper for a firm to give someone a computer and pay people to work at home than to rent huge offices for them to work in. With a computer and a fax machine, it's easy to keep in touch.

Then, again, there are all those people who work at home but don't get paid. How much do your parents get paid for cooking meals and cleaning up after you? When have you ever paid them for waking you up in the morning?

And, finally, there are millions of people who *do* go out to work but *don't* get paid. You are one of them. So is every other pupil or student in the land.

Some adults, too, go out to work without being paid for it. These are the people who work for voluntary organisations. They give their time freely because they want to help people. One 1980s survey showed that 8 in every 100 people do voluntary work in any one month.

citizens advice bureau

THE SALVATION ARMY

WRVS

The Samaritans

Voluntary work varies enormously. Some people collect money door-to-door; others keep telephone lines open or run charity shops. The Women's Royal Voluntary Service (WRVS) provides Meals on Wheels, runs clubs and does jobs for people who are housebound.

Why do they do it?

One of the oldest voluntary organisations is the Royal National Lifeboat Institution (RNLI). In fact, it's the oldest lifeboat service in the world. Since it was set up in 1824, it has saved over 122,000 lives.

In 1991 alone, it saved 1,308 lives – that's about three for every day of the year. In fact, extra leisure time has meant more people enjoy sailing or other sea sports. And more people need rescuing.

Lifeboats often have to put out in the worst weather conditions. The crew put their own lives at risk to save others. Over 400 lifeboat crew have died since the service began. But, with better boats, deaths these days are rare.

Most of the crews are volunteers. They do not get paid for saving lives. All they get is a small compensation for their loss of earnings while out with the boat. Who are these crew members and why do they do it?

The RNLI explains what sort of person serves on its lifeboats:

The mechanic is usually a full-time employee of the RNLI. The rest are volunteers. Teachers, engineers, fishermen, doctors – men and women from all walks of life are lifeboat crew members. In addition to their everyday jobs, they are ready to exchange the comforts of home for cold, wet, fatigue and possible danger. Whatever the weather, or the time of day or night, distress calls are always answered.

The children's programme, *Blue Peter*, has raised money for ten lifeboats. This one, at Portaferry in Northern Ireland, would now cost £56,000.

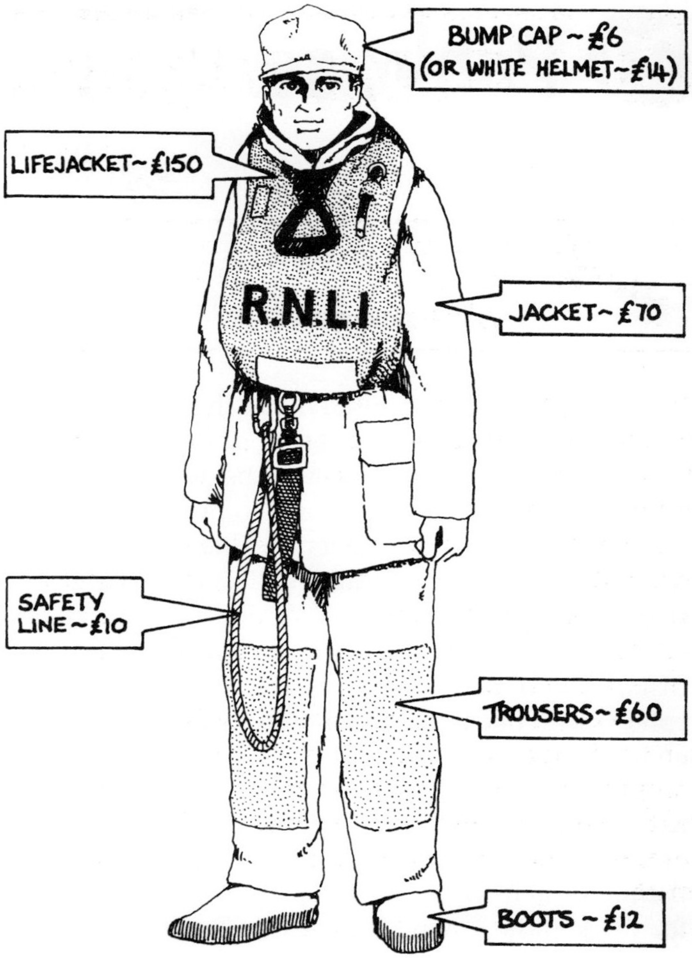

What it costs to kit out a lifeboat crew member.

Job sheet

1 a) Look at the lower drawing on page 42. Which do you think is the best reason for doing voluntary work – or doesn't it matter? Work out your reasons.
b) Read this page. What do you think makes a person want to be a crew member on a lifeboat?

2 a) Work as a class. Hold a brainstorm to come up with as many ways as possible in which you could raise money for charity.
b) Pick out the best 6–10 ideas.
c) Agree, as a class, on a charity to which you could give your money. (It doesn't have to be one on these two pages.)
d) Set yourself a realistic target: how much do you hope to raise?
e) Devise a plan for raising the money.

3 What do you think voluntary work has got to do with citizenship?

21 Public services

KEY *words*

amenities

It is a typical Tuesday in the life of the Patterson family. When they wake up, they don't rush around to check whether they've been burgled. They know there's a police force to protect them and their council house. Over breakfast, they listen to Radio 1 before the children collect their things together to set off for school.

The Pattersons live in a small village some distance from the school but a free school bus collects the children every day from a stop at the end of the lane.

Meanwhile, Mr Patterson puts the dustbin out because the binmen come on Tuesday. Mrs Patterson asks him to get some vegetables from their allotment on his way home. Then, he sets off for work at the Town Hall. He deals with the finances of local amenities, like the swimming pool.

Mrs Patterson works part-time in the children's section of the town library. It's her day off; anyway, she needs to see the doctor about a back injury. Her husband is convinced she's overdoing her judo training at the public sports centre.

Going into town on the bus, she passes the village hall. There's a big sign outside saying POLLING STATION. She had forgotten that it was the General Election. Not that she usually bothered to vote, anyway. It never seemed to make much difference who ran the country.

Job sheet

1 a) Which public services do the Pattersons benefit from?
b) Which ones are free?
c) Where does the money come from to pay for these?
d) Can you think of any reason why Mrs Patterson ought to vote? Explain your answer.

The Pattersons, like all of us, rely on public services. In some cases, like swimming pools, we have to pay to use them but many are provided free. Imagine a life without hospitals or ambulances, street lighting or proper roads.

In reality, of course, none of them is really free. The money must come from somewhere. Once you have a full-time job, your taxes will help to pay for all these services we take for granted.

Some of our free public services.

Job sheet

2 a) In groups, look at the drawings on page 44. Decide which services you think should be free.
b) Now, put them in order of importance, with the most important one at the top.
c) Compare your list with those of other groups.

In fact, the task of choosing the most important free public service is pretty impossible, isn't it? How do you choose between hospitals and schools, for instance? Without hospitals, the schools would be half empty because of crippling childhood illnesses. Without schools, no one would be educated enough to become a nurse or doctor.

Yet decisions must be made. The government has only a limited amount of money to spend. If it wants more, it must raise taxes – and most people don't like that very much.

That is why many public services are not totally free. For instance, it costs nothing to go to a doctor but, after your 16th birthday, you'll have to pay for a prescription.

Politicians argue fiercely about whether public services should be free – or about how much they should cost. So Mrs Patterson was wrong to think that a General Election made no difference. The government decides how much money is spent on each service – and each political party has its own priorities.

A new school being built. In this case, the Church of England contributed a lot of the money.

Job sheet

3 a) Copy out the grid below.
b) If you think a service should be provided free, write 'free' in column 1.
c) Now, decide how each free service should be paid for. Write either 'taxes' or 'charity' in column 2.
d) Compare your answers. How would you settle any differences?

Service	1	2
Refuges for battered wives		
Dental treatment		
Art galleries		
Ambulances		
Road cleaning		
Public libraries		
Kennels for abandoned animals		
Swimming pools		
Schools		
Youth clubs		

22 Citizens – young and old

KEY *words*

census trend Welfare State

Once every ten years, the government holds a census. This is a count of every person living in Britain. The government needs this information because it has to plan ahead.

In fact, the population of Britain has gone up only very slightly in recent years. In 1981, it was nearly 53 million people. By 1990, it was 57 million. So the government knows that it won't have many extra people to cater for.

But it's not just the total population which matters. Government ministers need to know roughly how many people there will be in each age group in the future. If the census shows there are lots of babies, then they may have to start building new junior schools.

In fact, the census has shown two interesting trends. The proportion of people under 16 is hardly changing. On the other hand, the number of old people is going up quite quickly. In 1900, only about 5% of people were old enough to have a pension (although they didn't actually have pensions then). Today, about 15% of the population is over 65.

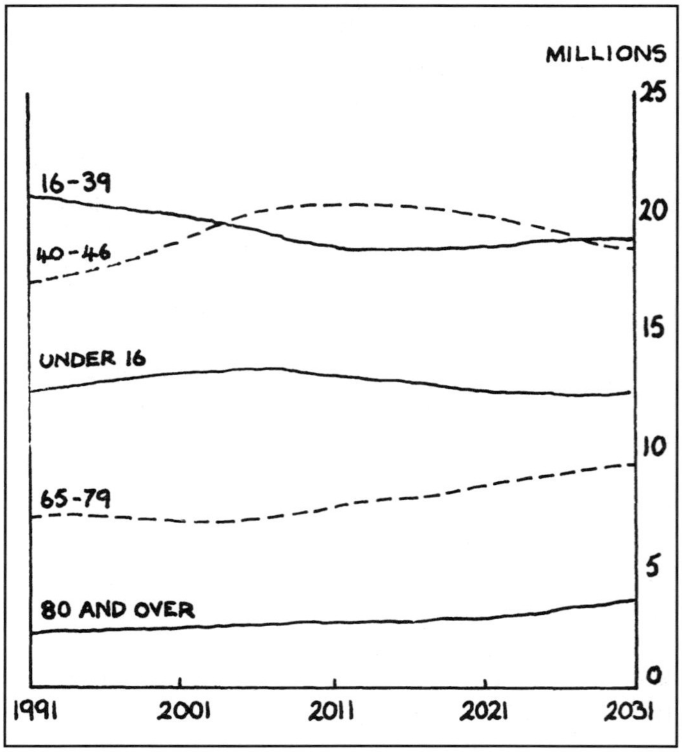

This graph shows you how the government expects the population to change in the near future. For instance, by the year 2031, it expects the number of pensioners to increase even further.

Job sheet

1 a) In groups, list all the needs of pensioners.
 b) Which of these does the government provide?
 c) Where does the money come from?
 d) Why will the number of pensioners affect *you*?

The Welfare State in Britain tries to help the old and sick, the young and the poor – in short, all those who cannot help themselves. The state looks after their *welfare*. There are few, if any, people who would disagree with this idea.

But all the benefits must be paid for. And they're paid for by people who are working. As you can see from the graph, the number of pensioners will go up, while the number of working people will not change much.

WHEN IT COMES TO PLANNING YOUR FUTURE

WHICH ONE ARE YOU?

In your lifetime, the government will have crucial decisions to make. Should taxes rise to pay for all the extra medical care which pensioners will need (not to mention all their pensions)? Or will state pensions not rise as fast as people might like?

And what about hospitals? Will people find that medical treatment is rationed? Will it become less easy to get a hip replacement (a very common operation for old people)? These will be decisions for politicians of the 21st century. And you will be the people electing those politicians.

And what about you? How will the country be doing when *you* reach retirement age?

Of course, no one thinks about retiring when they haven't even started work. But many people do not plan in their lives until it's too late. Some do no planning at all. But wise citizens think of themselves, as well as of their country.

The advertisement above was used by the Norwich Union to persuade people to save for a private pension. Governments, too, have encouraged people to start their own pension scheme. It provides an extra pension on top of the one provided by the state.

Will you start your own pension fund? If so, when will you do it? Or will you rely on the state giving you enough pension to live off when you reach retirement age? Or will you be one of those people who simply goes on working because they can't afford to stop?

These are the decisions facing you as a citizen of the 21st century. Being a citizen means you have rights and responsibilities. There are laws which give you rights and stop you interfering with other people's rights.

But there are no laws which tell you what decisions you must make in your private life. Your private life is your responsibility. And so, to a large extent, is what you make of your future.

Job sheet

2 Please work in groups. Discuss which of these things you think you should plan:
   a) your job;
   b) when you will get married;
   c) your birth control method;
   d) how many children you'll have;
   e) buying a house;
   f) what you'll do when you retire?

3 Look at the things you intend to plan. When do you think would be a good time to plan them?

Glossary

amenities – useful facilities
anti-social – opposed to the ideas on which society is based
bail – money paid to set a person free until their trial
bilateral aid – aid given directly by one country to another
bill – proposed law
Briton – British citizen
census – survey to get information about a country's population
citizen – person who is a member of a nation, by birth or choice
civil servant – public official, employed by the state
community – group of people who have something in common
conscience – sense of right and wrong
constituency – area which has its own MP
constituent – voter
constitution – principles on which a country is governed
contract – legal agreement
councillor – member of a council
damages – money paid as compensation for harm done to someone
democracy – government run by the people who live under it
democratic – following the idea that everyone has an equal say in decisions
dictator – person who has complete power
discriminate – treat differently
EC – European Community
election – choice of government by voting
elector – person who has the right to vote
enforcing – forcing (something) to happen
extended family – family which has more than just parents and children living together
General Election – election in which all MPs are chosen
Income Support – government help to those who need it because of inadequate wages
institution – organisation
juvenile – young person
libel – writing about someone which harms their reputation
lobby – try to influence MPs
Mace – symbol of power in the House of Commons
manifesto – statement of policies
minority – small group (less than half of the total number of a larger group)
monarch – king or queen
monarchy – country ruled by a king or queen
moral duty – duty based on what a person thinks is right
nation – group of people living in the same country
nuclear family – parents and their children
ombudsman – official who studies citizens' complaints against the government and officials, and recommends action to correct wrongs
Parliament – in Britain, the House of Commons and the House of Lords
perjury – lying in court
politician – person (like an MP) whose job is in politics
prejudiced – having an opinion without good reasons
remanded in custody – kept in prison
republic – country not ruled by a king or queen
resident – person living in a place
responsibility – obligation or duty
right – something a person is entitled to
slander – speaking about someone in a way which harms their reputation
stereotype – fixed idea about the qualities of a place or group of people or things
surrogate – substitute
tenant – person paying rent
the state – nation
tradition – long-time custom
trend – general direction
voluntary organisation – organisation run with the help of volunteers
voluntary work –work done by free choice, without pay
Welfare State – public services provided for the welfare of all citizens free of charge or cheaply